RING CYCLE

The long wait for a first full-length collection
from Alex Houen has been more than worth it,
it's been essential to the making of something
stirring, bothering, and confrontational, built with
artisanal skill. This is not a work stuck in imperialist
English, it reaches out, giving the 'sacred'
materials of Western thought an ironic workover
— sometimes with overt levity, sometimes with
self-mockery, sometimes with an intensity of
observation that floors you. Houen works with
that tangential 'voice' that claims no ownership,
no possessing. A tone book of word action!
— **JOHN KINSELLA**

EYEWEAR PUBLISHING

ALEX HOUEN

First published in 2018
by Eyewear Publishing Ltd
Suite 333, 19-21 Crawford Street
Marylebone, London W1H 1PJ
United Kingdom

Cover design and typeset by Edwin Smet
Printed in England by TJ International Ltd, Padstow, Cornwall

ISBN 978-1-912477-07-4

WWW.EYEWEARPUBLISHING.COM

for Isabella

Alex Houen
is author of the poetry chapbook
Rouge States (Oystercatcher, 2014), and co-author
(with Geoff Gilbert) of another chapbook, *Hold! West*
(Eyewear, 2016). He is co-editor of the online poetry
magazine *Blackbox Manifold* and teaches modern
literature in the Faculty of English, and Pembroke
College, University of Cambridge.

TABLE OF CONTENTS

I

Cry pretty, pretty, pretty and you'll be able
Very soon not even to cry pretty
And so be delivered entirely from humanity
This is prettiest of all, it is very pretty.
– Stevie Smith, 'Pretty'

RING CYCLE

Before, during, and after Anselm Kiefer

When I say *this high* I guess it is a salute
    to blobs of meat or blushing organs
and the height assumes a kind of blue-
    pink water minus Virginia Woolf.
Or when I say *this high* it is a salute
    of pale smoke baring face up to clouds
where clouds make faces palest sheets.
    Or when I make this salute it really says
NOTHUNG and is a voice inside singing
    EIN SCHWERT VERHIEß MIR DER VATER!
so I wonder blushing if my fire's collapsing
    back to water less Virginia Woolf.
Or when I make this salute suddenly
    there's a white cot in a wooden attic
this high. You can forget Virginia Woolf
    now when I say *this high* it really is
a salute to a closed forest of burning chairs
    minus the distance from it. For distance
is always packed with a kind of straw
    and often shot with a kind of lead
while my weapon of choice is *NOWHERE*
    to be seen. A woodcut is good for revealing
distance in a face. Or there's always the vast room
    that's departed long ago leaving bare
ruined lines to its vanishing point
    in the very air we breathe.
And when I say the air we breathe
    I really mean *this high* as a salute to stacks
of clay and lead and straw and books or
    shellac – though I'm really thinking of sulphur-
crested cockatoos perched on telegraph wires.

And I want to say *this high* is for those cockatoos
so when I make that salute it really prescribes
    tablets for anybody who wants them – tiny
cuneiform tablets to swallow into a building
    of real strength *this high*. And in building
that height I hope it's not a salute to the US
    Army's *COMPREHENSIVE SOLDIER AND FAMILY
FITNESS TRAINING* built to muster 'Total Fitness'
    in 'five dimensions of strength': physical
emotional, familial, social, and spiritual.
    Am I saying my weapon of choice is *BELIEF*?
For a salute made only *this high* surely shows
    where there's neither drone nor God appearing
to Abraham – only the very air we breathe
    as a vast invisible ziggurat of tiny cuneiform
tablets. And if *this time* I really want to be buried
    not in the kind of water that drowns out
its genitals but in the solid clinging earth
    shot with clay and lead and straw and books
it is only because the solid clinging earth
    is already so up in the air
hanging in the very air we breathe
    this high

BATTLESHIPS / ROMANCE

I

Spring out of touch makes the blood count for nothing,
Sugar. Till I saw you and felt an instant tense erase
all before me – a microwave pinging its chicken burrito
into adolescence. I am *so* entered a new phase
of the film about us. Imagine: me, rookie Captain
of an old destroyer playing at naval war games.
For ages I was run by a cleavage that kept my stoicism
hidden – from me and others. Now I must reveal it
to your father, the Fleet Commander, and you.
We'd all like to think I sail on Cicero and Sun Tzu;
for you remain ashore, encircled by a sandy halo,
driving our limbless veterans back to themselves.
We all have prostheses to bear – what else are emotions? –
and we must learn how to use them for combat.

II

Fight the enemy where he isn't. I'll show your father
we can beat the aliens that invade by our scanning technologies.
I first spy their craft: submarine skyscrapers that fly
and ruin our game. They seal us beneath a force-shield dome –
it feels like being held amniotically inside the death
of a triplet brother who was more mature than I am.
I keep seeing frogspawn, froths of washed-up surf,
then clusters of fiery exhausts, orificial and fatal.
Their weapons are heartbreaking, *unbelievable!* – though not
to my Japanese colleague, who stands for my imminent stoicism.
Here it comes, finally: when I prise off an alien's helmet
I see that he plays a team sport badly, he's huge and ugly,
he lives on equipment, he's denied the sun with his helmet.
Sun rising behind me, instant tense, I make him face me...

III

Those dull mangled noises he made – like an explosion
of old people, I'm told. I heard only a new voice
of responsibility singing its radar clear inside me.
When we chat online I mustn't forget that my face
came from someone who died. Indebtedness
to the dead; that's how our machines felt stronger than theirs.
Forget their hermetic force-shield, Baby;
forget them. You are safe on the island in touch with me
by satellite. Imagine your father awarding me
medals for saving the world with exposure to light:
men punching the air for days we can break together;
a photo of you, beating by heart, in a pocket;
and finally – *yes!* – my voice pitching in anew
with its bid for your hand and this being inside you.

HUÉ

it's good to be addressed as 'Alice' so close to the bone
/ here in Vietnam where every syllable houses different
tones / each tone its own meaning / so *ma* can be 'ghost'
'mother' 'tomb' 'that' 'horse' or 'burgeon' / the best kind
of family /

       in the restaurant of last night we ordered things
differently / tongue beef / rain sausage / sampled every
shingalingaling to its pageant / a Miss Universe parade
upon us / police keeping all but tourists in line with cattle
prods / Miss El Salvador waves right through me / Miss
Czech Republic smiles her deduction / crowd broken up
on local tv back in our hotel /

       we switch to a pirate dvd /
Shoot 'Em Up / cockney accents with weird English subti-
tles / 'my god' / *make hurt* / 'hugs and kisses' / *i guarantee
that* / ''e was a lousy tipper' / *he is British* / 'there's nuffin
on tv about this' / *do you like Taiwan casually?* / 'yer 9mm
is empty' / *you are the people I killed* / 'you know 'ow to use
this, right?' / *with it* / 'this is pretty fucked up' / *first and
so on* / 'thass quite alright, doctor' / *heed this Mr Facial* /
'forensic behaviour consultant' / *i do not hold hope* /

       next day
Ong Vu (Mr Rain) takes us to his home / explains oth-
er local investments / the annual death day feast / paper
scooters tvs and fridges burned as offerings to spirits / the
import of Hué as former capital / the import of burning
facsimile dollars not just for ancestors also ghosts of wan-
dering strangers / even GIs killed in the war / my atten-
tion wanders / delicious fishcake / that tiny frog by the
perfumed river / hiding from my hand in my hand /

       later
in the imperial citadel all bullet holes stay still as coy carp

feed on frenzy / somewhere JPAC teams are scouring hills for remains / seeking the right mitochondria to bury back in America /

tomorrow maybe we go to the man in the market and haggle for a silver Ganesha / it's been such a strange honeymoon / everyone keeps taking my hand / I am British / Australian / *with it?* / back home we'll help to amass New Year in the town square / city after city on big screens / texting with bits of ourselves / feeding our feedback / counting down hope with second hands / our turn to go up in smoke

I.m. Jon Plapp

*I shall consider human actions and desires in exactly the same manner as though
I were concerned with lines, planes, solids.*
– Benedict de Spinoza

VIII

Meeting you repeatedly at the Rivendell Child & Adolescent Unit
I came to see that every statement has the voice of an 'it' lurking in it.
Over a stretch of eight years I heard my words talk me into shapes
of conversation all about us – usually scraps, ragged as the torn sky-
blue ones which made up the Matisse acrobat hanging on your wall.

When on a ferry, stare at the swirls of wake, then at the metal floor beneath
your feet. The floor swirls. So did the leather floor of your room.

VII

Often when we met, that acrobat looked to be over everything in there –
an unfinished jigsaw of mourning. And you carried off such a gentle air
of being a third person with your wool ties and Humphrey Bogart features.
There was also something snowman about you, if a snowman is snow
that's content to stand for things that are out of its hands, like sun.

Can 'fate' be the name for a weather front of other people's feelings
you come to view as form of perishable dwelling?

VI

Down one side of your face ran a fine line that seemed neither scar
nor wrinkle. I never worked it out. Was it a mark of how you drew
out fears with calm expression? I tried to make my own face a mirror
in response, and felt flickering across it so many past scenes I couldn't
picture. I kept hanging from where my face was disappearing.

You slowly drew me out on whether I were folding my mother's pending
death into feelings for the girlfriend I couldn't fathom.

V

Silence is listening: when I began to admit it, you'd often talk of making
your abstract paintings and how, say, string tied across the canvas could guide
your hand enough while giving way to register your gestures' tiny waverings.
Most of your paintings' titles you took from poems by e.e. cummings.
By this stage your leather floor seemed a second skin to me.

All I could see of this was a mouth in the shape of a small house,
dissolving in time to the chants of black cicadas.

IV

One day I visited the gallery that held your work and I couldn't see
the link between cummings and your paintings – blocks of colour making
spectral shapes flicker electrically in the blank spaces between them. I stood,
silent, as I did years later when I couldn't believe the sight of those tiny
bubbles of eye fluid so clear against blue sky: division of internal moons.

'Clouds raining down (the upper bit) on man (the lower bit): it means
"To shake, to excite, to tremble." Ezra Pound translates it as "fortune"...'

III

Having married my girlfriend then left the country, that was me talking
through the Chinese character '震' to another girl who was under my skin.
I hadn't seen you for years, and I wish more of our talk had kept on sinking
in. Perhaps it has recently through the father I'd never expected to meet.
His voice and hands are foreign and mine – straight out of a novel.

I first took in that line on your face when you recounted an exchange:
'What do you want to be when you grown up?' 'A rabbit.'

II

That was the first thing that came to me yesterday when, out of the blue,
I received from an aunt your obituary. 'Parkinson's claims "artist
of emotion," Jon Plapp'; 'When the shaking caused by Parkinson's
proved too severe, he would place his canvases on the floor, leaning down
on his arms to hold them steady.' So, eight years of shaking hands with you

and I never noticed the change. Eight years of tearing fear into hours
and all that time it was you doing the trembling.

I

I know more now of your background life from reading your obituary
than I do from our years of talking. But I guess that's the point:
you performed an intimacy of abstraction as a gift, remaining
a stranger and on hand simply as the word 'it' or a scrap of blue paper
or piece of string or leather-covered floor. Through you I saw

how lives become things and things alive, and how a world can work
its way out of a labyrinth.

GOATSCAPE MONOLOGUE

When a society breaks down, time sequences shorten
by barter, insult, revenge, or neurotic symptom –
as when a man offers from his richest hand
a plastic bowl foaming with dew of daughter-
in-law, laughing, 'What law? What daughter?'
       From where the partition walls have been
demolished issue sweet smells of neglected infants
and the floury smell of pubescent boys' beds.
Foreign aliens imitate these beds for having none,
then day and night become confused, sun
comes too close to earth, and life turns
unbearable. Me, I tilled the garden of Grace
with its splendid trees and party of statues.
The tall neighbouring structures are collapsing
oversight. That exposed wall –
I break into a sweat then a run when I feel it all
at home in me. It conjures disaster as a date palm
conjures dates. For beyond the city wall it's not clear
that the roaming goats are goats.
Even the smallest goat may be a dreadful blend
of man and dog. I wouldn't know how
to broadcast their number for our dear children
of the cloud. Even without coupling,
the dogs found their folk like a 'big thing' –
a second head staring from behind your face,
your heart after you, beating its pulp.
They make room only for a single cause
to absorb all causality in their vision, everything
seen *as if*.
       As if: that was what I called it
when they stood around my bed, took my pulse,
crowned me with parsley to make sweet sport

of fears in a serving of time. Fear that if you fall
asleep some number will grow in your brain until
there's no space for you inside it fear that you lie
on a glass shelf of fear that you'll knock your bowl
from absent-mindedness or loneliness onto the glass
and break into screams and so fearful betray yourself
and speak those fears…

Their mixture of credulity and cruelty
has assumed the proportion of myth.
Under the feet of their leader the earth never grows
again; he need only be himself
to establish his enmity's third remove.
These days I see the very real power the right costume
can exert. I grow more and more daring:
pleated Persian trousers, sweeping cloaks, wraps, shawls,
veils, diadems with stupid expressionless stones,
even a carnival mask that reminds me of a dog we had
who behaved as though he wore one.

Memory is an unstable camouflage that grows
through the deadpan. Since envy and solidarity are better
than pity, I have offered up fire-free offerings to our
cumulus children again. They have come back to me,
as heavy a burden as ever. So our bonds of revenge
mature, and I see they have borne us
no reason at all to wonder.

OUARZAZATE

For Vahni Capildeo

so here i am / alone in the desert / taking time out of work / thanks be to you Ouarzazate for your empty 'Museum of Cinema' set against rosy dunes / Marrakesh went on and on about my confusion / iron kept in place by skin / vans made of saddest donkeys / orange blossom exhaust / pyramids of steaming snails / blood clotting my stomach / satellite dishes / monkeys in nappies / i kept thinking i'd find a prayer-raid shelter to write in / wrong wrong /

it's true i'm in good company / Ouarzazate / are you some kind of salvation jam? / the museum is full of all that left you alone in the end / there's not a screen in sight / the sets are empty / here a desolate village of Joseph that doubled for one in the *The Exorcist* prequel / there a chamber of Pontius Pilate and Asterix / here a fibreglass tomb of sparrows singing at hunger of two stray cats / all around are sands that staged New Mexican horror hills / the battle of Tafas / blood in Zucchabar / all so lone and level /

dearest Ouarzazate / i know you'll be happy to leave me keeping up a front / accepting some lot / thanks be to you for showing it's possible / back in Marrakesh maybe the waves and waves will set me adrift as a fibreglass skiff / wash me clean with sleep past worry / wash me clean past sleep / in the market of Jemaa el-Fnaa i saw an exhausted cobra sleeping in search of its fangs / a man selling second-hand human teeth complete with fillings / 'this one transmits BBC World Service'

NOT NOW, STELARC

Because I had administration on my mind
I didn't hear much of what my love said
on the phone before she touched an end
to the call and left me ringing with a note
of resignation so I went to an evening talk
by Stelarc with the hope he'd show me how
to make my mind up like a bed for strictly
liberated bodies – hot and scarred with tasty
repertoire of chimera. I even took some free-
style notes as what follows.
            To trigger fresh body we can turn stem
cell into sperm cell and further down
the line give it wireless contact lenses
with degradable transmission so the sex
becomes its own vision not unlike a poem.
Body can also be hung from hooks
to have a good view of police and threshold
heart beats amplified with a third
virtual hand programmed to be touched
involuntarily in Luxembourg performing
jerky little dance. After period consulting
stomach sculptures fashion 'wegs' from mini-
wings + legs to do their jerky little dance.
Implant scaffolding for ear to take root on back
of hand the scaffold made with relief for where
microphone will transmit Cyrillic pyewacket
kanji GPS for anyone online who wants to hear
a fist wave or fingers doing jerky little
dance.
            I sometimes think all writing is best thought
as letter-code recording of hands' jerky little
dance and typing quotes from it is therefore type

of tango? So what room for *emotion,* what for
romance? I ask Stelarc when his PowerPoint is over.
There's no call to privilege human *aliveness*
he replies – it's there even in puppetry or cat-
flap. Mind is simply body where body is
an object ripe for redesign.
            Back in my office I can't help thinking
that printing off a brand-new arsehole
might be a form of greed or nostalgia.
Or hysteria. Or hysteralgia.
A pale cross-section of sunlight on my desk
I read the text she sent after our last call –
a choked sob breaks out
cold and hard as you like.

ODE TO LIDIA VALENTÍN, WEIGHTLIFTER

Clean

I

Listen! I'm not talking a cake walk of 'strong men'
tottering as giant toddlers in car-shell dresses;
I'm not talking soft on the inside like Schwarzeneggy
when he punched that camel in the face as Conan;
I'm not even talking the perforated industry of bees.
No, I'm talking Lidia who proves beauty's never been
a floaty form that fits a concept with disinterest.
Beauty is a muscle of held breath lifting roots
of itself until a quantity of words or metal, say,
is made a personal best.

II

I don't know if it's a bit of death or some lost
cause that I've been grieving, but I'm taking heart
from the slo-mo asylum of your arms,
powering a sound-track of turbines, sirens
and creaking keels, as you thrust up
through the air's water before squatting
down in your own element and cradling
the bar to yourself. Now that's what I call
the beauty of *under-standing*: seeing a human
primed to burst free inside its own cells.

Jerk

III

So we're also talking anti-Tantalus:
not grapes or water out of reach, but causes
fleshed out and pushed to the level of effects
so a body may show how the surprising pauses
or lipstick it begins with may turn out to be 'will
to power' or a cloud by Gerhard Richter.
That's what I call the beauty of *up-bringing*:
surging to stand still as a war that's made
a monument from all that time running out
of you and into other people.

IV

It makes sense to exchange something absent
for something really solid and heavy,
and what a strange set of movements
you have to make to execute this present! –
one foot forward and one foot back,
arms raised victorious in surrender until
you can gather yourself to stand for it
and finally give it up. Watching you
I fucking love my life – and so it drops
back into place, falling happier once again.

ANIMATION

A month of being forced to perform an Oedipal shuffle
(I sprained an ankle on falling drunk from my bike)
and now here I am in an alpine hotel; bedridden,
making collapsible mountain after cliff after mountain
with my knees beneath the sheets. With each seismic
shift the window's biopsy of sunlight shows me
a snap-shot of shoddy still-life, while my head
casts itself the shade of a head-shaped cloud.

Across a valley of the bed you are sleeping
with your viral fever. What a pair we make.
Outside, the rest of our party must have joined
the joy-wishers in throwing themselves down slopes
for real. So many iron filings on a sheet
of paper, a cluster of magnets under it drawing
them all around – that's a vision of not looking
out the window. I've just left my father's

Christmas (it's New Year's Eve) and I can't work out
the scale I have of things. A miniature black
plastic Christmas tree has grown as fragile in stature
as the street lights here which hang like huge crystallised
bronchioles of public lungs. Yes, that's also
a vision of not looking out the window.
It's this list lying discarded between us on the bed
that's keeping me from looking – the list I made

of souvenirs my father has collected over years.
Last night I found myself turning them into a kind
of doll of him in my mind. The two Ethiopian
earspoon crucifixes became his feet; the brass
callipers his legs; the tiny rusted dagger

(Moroccan) did for his genitals, while his portly torso
was the crucible ('AD 1770') stuffed
with organs of astrolabe, jade polar bear,

and abacus. Two mini vices were his hands, hovering
around him, armless, as if remote-controlled
by the obsidian figurine of his head – carefully sculpted
to be a penis, cat, or woman's face depending
on the angle from which you regard it. And after all that,
could I get the thing to work? No, it's useless,
and I've no instructions apart from his badge declaring
'Seniors Do It Better'. There was nothing left

but to place each piece of him back within its perimeter
of dust. So: have I committed anything at all?
If not, it's amazing how stern the sleeping back
you've turned to me looks. You're so riddled with the morning's
light it's terrifying. And I dare not answer you,
most beautiful sphinx, in case you wouldn't devour
me if I got it wrong. When I finally look out the window
it's iron filings, paper, and magnets all the way.

Something inside me growls its sigh of relief.

ALEXANDER'S FASHION FEAST

After John Dryden and Alexander McQueen

I

Ice floe slowly slowly slowly
blue-noir feedback screen reveals
cross between Venus and Medusa
writhing naked ecstatic in sheets
for these first models of a future
not to materialise again
igneous fear and audience with breath.

> It's frozen. It's alive. It's frozen. It's alive.
> So the runway is drawn by faces
> of diamonds. The screen gone all Rorschach.

II

We could name this restaurant 'Noah's Ark'.
Here's one swathed in a single bolt
of her own skin grown in a culture.
Ventral digital print of boulder-
brain coral drawn in to an empire
waist. Hair Cadillacquered into two
fins for echoes of feedback loop.

> 'A felt emotion is a conquered emotion.'
> We must take on each facet separately
> with both sides of our face like a fish.

III

Now is one with diamond's indifference.
Shell-petal armoured corset
wasp-nipped waist and leopard shark
jodhpurs. Thick onyx neck-

band for a free-floating head
bandaged with balaclava of sea
lace. Surely she's living on herself?

> It's live. It's numbered. It's live. It's numbered.
> Each model an air of carrying
> a spare pair of herself inside her.

IV

Here are some with evening-bag
stomachs grown from scaffold and stem cells.
Paniered damask pettiskirts. A lavender
bladder ditty bag. Buskins
of honeycomb stingray. Jerkins
of torpedo scad. Capes of Manta
for heaven's sake! The care is in the pleats.

> 'Always feeling and illusion were warring
> in me.' Each model wearing her mouth
> parting squid-ink lips.

V

Another sequence wanting no
conceit? A piano fangblenny
abaya shredded down from the hips.
Nude fabric peplum tops
and blade-fire-coral appliqué.
Golden crinoid epaulettes. This one
naked but for mother-of-pearl squamation.

> It's alive. It's numbed. It's alive. It's numbed.
> Each model some coral beneath the skin.
> 'We must conquer our geometrical completeness.'

VI

Can the pity of it blaze to love?
Can there be accessories to love?
Here are black ghost knifefish gauntlets.
A sand-dollar mosaic breastplate.
Apotropaic anemone amulets.
Here are models betraying no difference
between deep sea and feedback screen.

> The last models are more alive
> than anything living. Their bodies loaded
> with diamonds to remain unburied.

VII

Unburied even in so living it
with glacial slowness. For where I have
experience is an image of a mouth frozen
unsound undone unfound undergone
breathing nothing saying nothing
leaving nothing but a pool of black
ink or critical pupil watching me
inside hanging by an obscene thread
what was my former life dear life
now is making homes in surfaces
as fearlessness is Gorgon shield of conscience
so I make my best decisions
less my own and more for hunger

> hunger for a sound mouth a sound
> mouth in tender things fleeting
> once and for all.

ILIAD KID I

A rewriting of Curzio Malaparte's 'Iliade Infantile, I' (1939)

The boy watches the valley, green olives alight in the wind,
    towered town bristling with smoking chimneys,
loved-up horses gambolling by the river,
    all the alarm at the heart of him transmuting
into a neighing of white foals weighing up the air.
    Sad and lonely he listens for the sex of factories
that pours between white sheets hung out to dry.
    A dusty taxi blares radio down the mountain pass
where pine logs used to pass for a transport
    of funeral pyres. A pedestrian estate agent bares
his whitened teeth for a cleaner passing by.
    Soldiers by the playground laugh shields of air
against the view of other cleaners who bear rumours
    between them as dead-weight of linen –
a white armour crushed to slender hips,
    bare arms, and necks.
The boy hears the plain sad whine
    of a train remote as control. Already,
autumn's patrol is turning memory back
    to empty cicadas clinging to black vines.
The fields remain a close shave.
    The sky's hem is still white as a sheet.
The steeple is a metronome frozen in spite
    of the wind.
                The girls have other eyes,
other mouths, other sources, their voices cleaning up
    after those countless voices that scraped up
all the adolescence.
    Now the boy is alone, is over the sweet season
of races, hide-and-seek, and games
    with burnt offerings. Crickets are singing

buried in red sunset, and the horses are neighing
    on the hill under the first stars ever.
All the alarm at the heart of him sounds
    a death-wish: to die hanging by the neck
from a tight cord of sympathy –

    until he has his head in a book again
and sees just how stingy death is.

GETTING AWAY WITH IT

I

I rise 6:30 sharp; my father's at the window,
his fake begonias framing the view.

I join him, hoping Monte Bianco will bite off
more than we can chew.

We flesh out silently as somewhere sun
muscles in across the peaks and roofs:

a faint rose glow starts to dawn
on the town casino.   Rose turns gold.

More gold.   Gold turns to glare.
More glare.   There, it's done –

time to get away with the morning.
His dressing gown undone,

I spy the nitroglycerine patch he's wearing
for his heart.   Frustration is my darling.

II

I'm standing, he's sitting, and once again
it's time to bid our wishes and goodbyes:

he rises slowly from his chair and then
we bump into each other

left-side chest to left-side chest, then
right-side chest to right-side chest

as though we each switch for a new line
to read beyond the other.

This embrace lies somewhere between
commuting, Sumo, and jumping

to conclusions. We first met when I'd passed
twenty-seven years, so now to him I'm fifteen.

I would rather adapt a child than get it.
No getting around the fact: it was perfect timing.

SOILED *TU*

as if your name meant *once* / for all / a gallery
hanging in drizzle so long ago / so sick of all in-
voluntary flashbacks of you / cobblestones folding
to field / baroque / a walk in the Peaks / bidden
not by madeleines but accidence / a crow in a cage
crowing bait for a fox / you woke in a choke asking
if you'd spoken your sleep / our cupid called 'none
of the above' /

        it's only next day i realise / no /
you'd already gone and i'd been reading always
sheets of news to block the view / i called it com-
posure for getting ahead / as if your name meant
once / to hell with it / let's call this state a trip to
Pompeii / my face stuffed with *carciofi* / *penne arra-
biata* / *Macedonia* /

        a guide appears and forges ahead
/ now here is bloodstone pigment on plaster / here
where wool was softened in urine / there a local
plastered skeleton in glass-casing facing a hunting
fresco / here a girl with no nose begging / is there
such a thing as second nature? / blushing / your
smile a simile / an allergy you had to feeling on the
face of others /

        now here is macaronic wall of plas-
ter and lava in need of some facing / ready to flesh
out / that immaculate lamb-skull back in the rain
/ let me view you then / holding the glass case of
your hand / as if your name meant once / your ben-
ediction / let go my hand to this / a composture
/ my attention falls on graffito / a winged phallus
crumbling fast asleep /

now i'm back in the field ob-
serving a pitch-black creature / looks like a
moth / no / a crow / no / a spreading slick of
eye oozing into the lushest valley /

what vow
was broken there? / those times we snuck into
knick-knack shops to snap off the heads of por-
celain figures / i so can't be composed / may-
be i will be back in Naples / back in the Royal
Palace where 'Psyche' is an ormolu sideboard /
its mirror bearing your face / bait for what you
damned well have to see

79 SANDFORD GROVE ROAD

and I

Lived on, flew on, in the reflected sky.
— Vladimir Nabokov / John Shade, 'Pale Fire'

A whorl and delta, a winged fingerprint of flight
    dead against glass.
Only the eye on the pane has left no impression
    of taking place,
and the smudge of wings is still imploding into
    that glancing void.
On the path below, a few feathers betray
    their alibi. The only
other sign of a body is me leaving
    my breath to vanish.

If a mirror is a window with some sort of backing,
    this window is a mirror
there where its spectral sketch of bird
    draws me starkly
to times when my face has suddenly ghosted itself
    to a flashback;
times when its expression hovers out of sync
    with what I meant;
times when my voice is my mother's, say, my face
    emptying through it.

What doesn't leave a smear behind as testament
    to giving life
to transparency? This window's glaring blank of an eye,
    apparently. That's
where the window and loss of bird still promise
    some shared vision

of a death that can occur without a body –
      the ultimate crime.
Or grief. If only I'd been down on the path to help
      the dove to its feet.

Then it wouldn't have ended with my cat
      getting its tongue.

STRANGE MEETING

For Ai Weiwei and Davide Castiglione

Here I am, floating free
    of the whole free love thing, suffering
severe concussion of a little history
    turned personal. Nothing
concrete about that. Nothing concrete
    in wanting to be a lovely surgeon
making lovely loop-holes beat
    deep inside a body that's been searching
how to make a new sacrum
    outside itself for a 'dainty bit' of sacrifice.
Or how to turn a tangled bracken
    of reinforcing steel bars into a straight face
that's never occurred to you.
    I am somewhere between
name and number, and I try to
    imagine myself between
name and number. This is what I call
    making friends
with severe concussion. If my facial
    expression is a marble field
of grass, that is so it recalls the rubble
    and can continue long without me;
can continue to double
    for so many fingers raised to the CCTV
inside that scours the intimacy of the internal
    and infernal as one organ;
can continue to perform with no scalpel
    my beauty work as lovely surgeon
pursuing any sign of D. H. Lawrence.
    Look – twilight filling shrubbery with incarnate fury.

I love how what's properly useless often happens
      to grow into an alternative day buried
unreckoned in a little history. And how
      that extra day can grow into a setting,
placeless, solid, bright, and crowded
      as an airport terminal. Eating
there with a hunger you can't fathom
      feels *de rigueur*? So I eat to the letter
of the comrade I imagine –
      the stranger the better.

TWO TO TWOMBLY

Clay mound sprouting poppy pods
                         won or lost by bidding
we're ditching Gaddafi
                sorry   no   Cavafy
not over arch nor kind
    of 'synchronous face'
                       so I see already I'll end
in flashing martial art a
     No   each form does not call
for a Gaddafi drawn in hideous chariot
    by immortal pensive steeds
grave still before a quote before the best horse
    crossed out something tragic.
I know my fate   not to fall even
    but sad   not acutely but cutely
grievable while longing a long clip
    of ammo to wind about my head
in way of seasoning   To count for others   on others
    To see them shot through with a *KISS THIS*
amassed & harnessed internally as an Achilles
    thing scrawled like a cock.
               No wonder I am untraining my best
               hand to be discharged in manner
               of a classic 1962 claw that can do good
               watch face.
    Watch: the Achilles thing
furied & hairy now with close-range blood
    raising medium-range blood
      No   not simply monument nor moment
not mental metal nor mantle
              MANUMONUMENTAL?
Un-name of violence improper it's a disaster

exhibits the artist biding some head
to show heart-shaped buttocks making thunder
a brevity of arse rolling lotus flower
shaped willy-nilly of shit.
A bird's-eye view grows out of it
to battle synopsis of stationed forms
junking location to throw gravity
tanks drawn of attention
So ill I am.
The date is a cloud   and shade –
you are not Cavafy shading Gaddafi
you are not Alpha come over all Delta
nor bleached beached memory.
Send me my scrotal chariot plus thrower
of flames not to be confused
with sublimity.   I've tried so hard to fist
this response to myself   grasp
that funereal minimalist fist
a forum in its own right
a forum like a shield unfinished
as a mirage against some dunes.
So we made this box of dunes
& stuffed it with their stuff only to get
the right *AIM* obscene
for shit was always Paris's
best plaster   the whole thing
smeared off-white to bear this graffitaph

DEAD AS A GIFT
SNAFU
TO REMEMBER US BY
IDEAS CAN NEVER CLAIM

AN UNPAINTED SACRIFICE BY J. M. W. TURNER

The greater the distance, the more landscape
cooks up horizon to a light clumped so close
it broke into my home to live on and on –
a hungry angelic orphan
smouldering as a household sirocco.
It will never be all voice and no body.
The more I gazed,
the more it seemed to speak nothing
but swelling demands:

>   *Clasp me speechless, lend me your ears*
> *and I'll make you numberless days*
> *rising over a scumbled lake where even a skiff*
> *of compunction is barely discernible.*
>   *Commit me your duty –*
> *I'll consign you painstaking focus*
> *for any city to feel oblivious*
> *and full of the best cattle and sheep.*
>   *Give me your sheep and cattle*
> *and I'll render you cloisters*
> *of water where everywhere tension*
> *converts to calm skin of reflection*
> *to show you the softest durable Venice.*
>   *Have you ever witnessed a crypt*
> *without depth? Give me your Venice,*
> *I'll make you incredible morning toast*
> *of mountains spread with golden voice*
> *of all you love most.*
>   *Do you think you hold no price?*
> *Tender me what you love most*
> *and I'll make it happen purely*
> *as priming of canvas for cobalt blue,*

white lead, rose madder, and chrome yellow —
all to burst into paradise…
    And so it went on, until I made my face
a death-mask. Then I reached for a palette knife.

AFTER A LINE BY JOSHUA CLOVER

For Geoffrey Gilbert

'I like the Canto where Ezra tries to fuck a rock.'
Last night, mashed in Bar Rosa Bonheur,

Geoffrey and I realised everyone just needs a bit
of their own death and then to see their friends. Today,

he's off to the library for a bit, so I'm off to Palais
Galliera to make a nest of Jeanne Lanvin dresses

on display – *Salammbô, Walkyrie, Bocage, Hérissée,*
Polaire, Lavande, Rarahu, Phèdre, Outremer,

Mensonge, Sèvres, Alcmène, Lesbos, Fouquet's,
Donatienne, Mélisande, Fusée, Cyclone, Les Éclairs –

a nest to doze in a display of common luxury.
'You'll drool on them,' says Geoffrey.

'*You'd* drool on them,' I say.
'I'd have a wet dream in them. It's my fashion.'

I like the Panto where Geoffrey tries to fuck a frock
(*en taffetas de soie gorge-de-pigeon*).

ANTENATAL WARD

The space between two bodies
is called an 'anaesthetic'
not a 'screen'.

In this paper suite of heart-
beats I read a young man
was average height

only to become this size
on the battlefield. Something
about someone throwing

bananas at his speech –
a metal shiver shoots
down each leg

charged less with violence
than its capacity
to go on holiday.

Each morning I add honey
to a broom-handle's tip
to save an exhausted

bee from our kitchen sky-
light. 'Are you leaking out
more than usual?'

Have I underpaid in blood?
Arch your back again
my sweetest heart

I'd break my mouth of glass
if it could make an exit
with your pain.

II

The wounded fall in the direction of their wound…
– Lucretius

SPHERE

'A rapey month of little walks' she jokily
pronounced this time, but it didn't stop there;
it's like a distended accident – that instant
between knowing you will crash and actually
slamming into metal rolling on and on
until a massive shiny sphere rippling mercurial
gathers space as living room and gives
the impression that to be thrown is to be
newly-born, descended from oneself.
As anxious curiosity becomes a form of genital
the sphere was throwing broken voices back
in heaps to keep us both absorbed in its domestic
plunge. It was perfect for a while:
'Here, Sweetie,' I said, as I heard it in my head.

Sometimes it gave a kind of raptor coo.
I could also hear distant ocean in the shallows
of its breathing. But there was something martial
in the mix of its absent- and bloody-mindedness.
Every time we gazed on it it rolled
around its surface dimpling reflections
of what we could have done until we felt utterly
submerged – 'asleep with a million jelly fish
in a neon tank of time-being.'
Drifting tranquillised can be a good thing.
As a child I was teased by older kids who said
if I closed my eyes and tried hard enough
I could see through flesh. I cried purely
because despite their lies I knew it to be true.

We were having silences that wouldn't settle
for the sphere. Echoings and croodlings turned
to muffled straining – as though every hour
triggered off some bowel. I know now
that in the beginning was not a word but a tone.
Yet at the time I could barely distinguish the sound
of bees in honeysuckle from flies in the corpses
of frogs. We needed a broader concept of imminence;
something of the sphere was oozing subcutaneous
and we couldn't tell just what. I suggested some poetry
could make nothing happen for a while. Not enough,
Honey, she said; write it like it never happened.
Like it never happened. For existence is believing
you know whom you love, and what does the loving.

INFANCY AS HISTORY

I have a daughter
But no child
– George Oppen, 'Of Being Numerous'

thrown to 'self' to be un-
thrown yet throwing self
at all that someone
      so much there
is present face as barest
      wave or pear hand
      drops to pear so made
is inner thumb and index
finger at a pinch to hold
      a single kidney
      bean
up to power face
      open
as cut grass

      ★

Darling we are living in a time
      I doubt we can say age
featuring a single-season tv character
whose super-chipped brain can roam
online to make calls hack data
      while he wanders inside a photo
      even seeing to the back
of its faces then its history.
I think he can extract future
      from furniture
      a man from a mango
such is the disbelief suspended

by his agency as countless bound
headlong villains

★

asleep face down to an app
of ocean sounds on loop
          Dear Eyes
beware of sparrows on a guy wire –
mortgage in disguise

★

I believe your laughter in my head
dropped onto the arm of a chair
displays your knack for circumstance
and how you wear it camouflaged
in eating it as all desire is bound
to be pantomime of inanimate things
taking your time to make alterations
          even in spinning a plastic navy
          lid is no information
for the best things these days
hold something intensely involuntary

★

who says a capacity to do something
holds the capacity not to do it
when London is next to Beijing
and the city can instil so much
difference in occupation between
          bidding and biding
          suspense and boredom
          manicure and manure.

For Matthew Miller Spring/Summer
2014 'modernised the demob suit
silhouette adding oversized pleats
and attaching shredded fabric
      in a death-rose embroidery
      on plethora of blue hues
      and mashed-up pinstripes
to look like a walking battleship'

*

I watched you so happy on this beach
afternoon surrounded by balconies
      pieces of sea-glass in hand
bobbing in your yellow plastic chair
      I blew up with my breath

                heavens!

wave upon wave of you
taking no prisoners

LETTER TO A NEIGHBOUR

door ajar / summer flies / this room a stride / you cross
my mind / free from the funny farm or on parole again
/ vandalising your own home as i speak / what mouth
has ever sealed a roof inside its head? / i see your point /
a house needs breathing space / japanese knotweed may
indeed spread to a wall between itself / between what
is too fast to forget / too bare to remember / an open
secret plan adjoining flash-backs / yes i see / building a
cave could be a breeze if nowhere looms an absolute for
absolution to ablute / and tomorrow your breeze-block
toilet plan will draw the invisible boundary line you're
building / the line we say we sanction /

                                 when i asked a
friend how much to shoot you in the head i thought i
was joking / a walrus moustache sunning itself in your
front trench / freedom puppetting the way a home and
what it's not abrade each other suddenly as laughter /
your red laser gunsight unzipping my living room wall
/ between itself / between /

                              between you and me i ac-
tually think i could fall for your demolition / recall my
share of mortgage a friend injected at a fixed rate / teen-
age years returning with a dream of home / the back
half built of something with a shelf life of canned fruit
/ so we coughed and coughed to hack up our tangible
architecture / a viscous skeleton standing for air / blue
pink / sinking hands / plughole eyes / i'm so still in the
face of it i feel you dislodging inside / bearing earth
from around your foundations in search of blood wav-
ing its little white dress / as long as need be / the life led
there to be spent /

i even like your idea of swearing as a conservatory / red white orange muscles of carp rippling up an internal pond / orchids and fly-traps / humid heat of speech / the slew of stones it warms to host / yes / so many an eye outlives its socket / and what is a promise if not a ghost? / that's the genius of your planned extension cave / transcendence is no planning permission / what is a sun if not its removal? / discarded earth core / grey breeze weed / flies / your body yoked to a shadow / discharged

GEOMETRIES OF MEMORY

There is no document of civilization which is not at the same time
a document of barbarism.
— Walter Benjamin

Backing vocals upside-down to war
    bone-white stucco ceiling cupids
gunning for wings against memory
    folded as working pockets.

★

A crimson ceramic sea or carpet
    of marginalia making a tower stand
for so many unknown names
    visible from 50 miles or so.

★

Human wings consolidate reversible
    flesh to field and persuade others
with a pattern of good grief
    mostly looking down.

★

As people descend into this monument
    their heads disappear
when their hands touch names
    below eye level.

★

Such memory is lovingly vertical
    just as what's remembered is named
and so horizontal. Holbein's ribs
    keeping the corpse propped flat.

SMOOTH GLOSS FINISH

Imagine a pair of dead-locked wrestlers, stalemating
for hours on end because family is cause,
effect is ageing, and thickening of necks
yields data. Such suspension is heat,
in which the intimacy of those who make up plans
of common works is rediscovered.
                                    Changing tires,
piercing an abscess, keying a programme –
it's easy to manage a limited operation
if you can substitute something like a 'living statue'.
The organisers have scrambled special huts.
Imagine an immense crowd assembled in hope
of witnessing a bull-fight in a ring that's far too small.
Near-and-far smells of plaster, pelts, wax, smoke,
screens, oiled locks, and indoor palms.
Nothing but evening in here for the audience;
out there, a summery river lustrating itself
past shutters. Above all else, some spirit
must be mustered so the statue can be vehicle
and audience possible – then all the occasion's intensity
is concentrated and let loose
in little cakes.
                    A hoof raised in the economy of fear,
the young statue's hide runs like water
gone somewhere terribly fast yet trembling still
under the hand of 'The Butcher'.
His beauty lies in the audience avoiding his gaze.
His flesh exudes a perfume of fungi,
a captured dampness held by a frame
broad, porous, and sleep-worn, as if sleep
has been angling for fear. The unendurable
always kick-starts a curve of audience joy,

for eating an exotic species is the best luxury
of feeling death isn't even necessary.
As a satyr is neither man nor beast deprived
but hunger pressing its breast to prey,
so statue and butcher consummate seasons
of hope this evening. Sweet immortality
of habit, the young statue's mind
harbours a vivid plan of road network, river-
line and mountain range. The butcher must keep
distance spaced fine as a salad to touch the unbroken
animal – what's before him is never less
than husbandry.

An amputated hand cannot be
disowned for holding futurity, and the audience swarm
with exchanges: 'where's his stand?'; 'is that mascara?';
'the posture's awful'; 'he's diving into memory';
'he's gone for total realism'...

The butcher seems drunk with the youth, an embryonic
ship in a bottle. Never having met, they already share
a phantom history of domestics, excuses,
and merry-go-rounds of bingeing. These excesses
of life-force, which locally block the poorest economies,
are in fact the most dangerous factors of ruination.
'Relieving the blockage' was always the end
of this feverish pursuit 'in the darkest region of consciousness.'

Plan was to gainsay excess with a series of easy extractions:
A statue from statutes. Awe from a drawer.
Some lag from flag. The juice of justice.
Salvation from salivation. Ending
from the pending.

See how the horizon catches light sound of propellers.
How skin contains responsibility.
How skin is of fire.
As a gun barrel's surface reflecting a scene
adds to the scene some realism, the butcher shows

with a blow how the audience draws a new-born
with all its bellows and calling.
                              The next season will feature
various out-takes, including an Arctic woolly-bear
moth that completely freezes each winter, thaws
each summer, until as a fourteen-year-old larva
it finally mates to die.
                              I'm lucky to have this permanent job.
Some of these folks have been raised almost entirely
on live feed.

THE IDENTIFICATION

this morning my face is not to be seen in the motel mirror / some film in its place screening as steam / thinking rooms come fully furnished with yourself is mirror's auto-cue / a floating me you appear to slip on like a name or face to assume yourself ossified inside / sound / safe / buried in an open album / no key to the skeleton you have / have never met / no key for your ears' ossuary / its buried sound / dreams of personal archaeological digs / so the world turns flat again /

winter and winter passes spring / the tension pulpable / but this morning has hit on some shift key / everything in the room turning a gaze to white gauze against its window / crickets coding heat outside / getting away with your hearing / feels like loss / loss in the form of friendship /

as day goes by the loss is more than it was outside / something in here tapping / i've heard such feelings make a hard case for a person / this must be a good film / *noir* / to occur to us now an event must make its impression under cover of darkness / Alain Delon's secret pockets / a bikini of trees / a glass of helmet / suspension as form of solution / sentenced / feeling itself to be

here / maybe now some face is prepared to make its entrance? / and when i do even the street will be in it / the one i've been avoiding / the street of my friend / open as fire / smoking inside me / bringing a little life to my life / so i see him now / now as then / i'll even pay him in visits / now watch me put out his hand before i know it

FOURTEEN WAYS TO WEIGH A HAND-SHAKE

For Matthew Bevis

Only truthful hands write true poems. I cannot see any basic difference between a handshake and a poem.
– Paul Celan

I
on the other hand when I offer
    my *Here I am* as *Here*
you are I show my hand
    grasps neither weapon nor poem
while shaking happens to seal
    a hidden empty chamber

II
every handshake blossoms
    an event incarnate and never
contemporary with the world
    in which it takes place   a touch
of agapemone

III
and this space   this floating digital
    vault forms an irregular
globe of forgetting   fleeting
    and persistent as Christmas   or a football
of No Man's hand

IV
so give up some person
    parting lips by what's held
to dwell in common   globular

inflorescence of onions
splayed garlic stalks
    seeds of the umbelliferous
swallows drawing cracks
    through Lalique enamel ocean
bats eclipsing diamonds
    a swamp surface glitters
all these present gestures
    we may now call hospitality

V

pitch cenotaphic space
    unbreathable   unheard   unseen
a ventricle neither mine
    nor yours nor wholly here
to bid both greeting and
    goodbye

VI

if I can't hear my thoughts for shaking
    how can I tell what hand
I'm dealing?

VII

make a warm marmoreal surface
    hold fast between heroic
labours of Venus and indifferent
    fall and rise of ocean
to mollusc over agreement

VIII

slipping unconscious a little
    limp death in a bid for a plot
of planet before it burned
    and cooled into sea   land

plants   beasts   relations
    machines   the dullest socialites
feel a shiver divining
    such congratulations

IX
shake   same

father's   lover's

sake   shame

X
press yourself a share
    of flesh   on the line as on hold
a cocoon of cash where flesh is
    valued to fix its departure
handmade and unsigned

XI
whistling bits of metal
    all around I go
composed through one well-executed
    move and sense that Fortune
only had the smallest paw
    in turning this humane

XII
a lost space capsule opening
    on one hand taking on the other
a little impersonal life
    speaking of rain or good weather
in a dead man's room   where
    the accent's from   no idea

XIII

a cell shaking so
    to speak with its bank I sink
to its havoc as any fiction is
    always upheld by contract
playing at fitting in figures
    of sleep   to leave you all
the stranger

XIV

a moment's disbelief at having come
    to grief   a new amnesiac
shaking   an instant clump
    of airborne afterlife   hanging on
and so mistaking us home

FROM A RESTING WORLD

A rewriting of Curzio Malaparte's 'Da Riposati Mondi'

From a resting world her voice
calls its oyster, tenderest
anxiety to face those wounds
waiting to happen as after-
shave boxed with ribbon.
Sometimes singing in the shower
is not speaking inside, a form
of suicide with so many tiny
fingers. Old mirror
was happily a kind of credit
card that will end perhaps
in floating past error. The garden
these days sees no change
between hanging baskets of god
and marigold. Something to do
with children. Dear High Truth
or Fate (same thing) go fuck
yourself by the lip of our girning
cliff and wait for your lack
to grow shoulders and wings. No
one will be expecting it again.
Like powdered beef and eggs
the measured fauna in our heart
and kids against the pride
in civic plaques. No secret
can resist the pride of people
chained to rock by the lip
of the cliff that's everywhere.
We are so fixed I crave
a spare exterior tongue

to grow safe in its nacre.
With people this valid you have
a volcano stoking us up
a beauty only for humans
and concept void. So when
I have the pleasure of being
hit with disinterest I must be in
common? This morning many are
clearing it of world while buying
hosts of endless objects:
wire, crustaceans, wallpaper,
parrots – all for one buttery
spread of land. The light
shed by back-up headlines
brooks no looking back.
Tiny numbered flecks
of spit sizzle on night sky.
So no change between altitude
and attitude, and the new constellation
is called Head of State. Unexpected
fear as sudden event:
the shot came from anywhere at any
time in any form.
When oversight can take a spill
again it will be so so
gorgeous. No one will know
how the flight will have fallen into
her lap full of pets and people
waiting to happen. Her screech
is of brakes wild with unknown
reproduction. When you've taken
this altitude on board and eaten
it, sleep will give you a softer
naked body as landing.
All those secret folds
to hold the flight in place.

WINTER SOLSTICE NOCTURNE

That bronze, hollow statue of Diana made a hive
    by bees bearing summer's end – was it with someone
else's eyes I saw her? I see her now
    hunting down a stash of light for winter, second-hand,
glowing to the shortest time of day: a snap-shot.
    Outside, some trees are holding breath and nothing
is decorated for its service.
    The river has fast been turning depths to surface
like a face frozen by an unplanned parting
    kiss. Now the river is an image of her face snap shut
on all the times we had together, so I can understand
    how her eyes have carried into mine and shadow
all I see. Even our furniture feels so struck by separation
    that tonight's both latent and alive with me its captive.

It's when I fully realised how she raised me with love
    for death that I began to love those things
that seem to hover on a cusp: volcanoes, coral,
    statues, flame trees, Mannerism, stalactites,
the sun, bees, scaffolds, windows, film sets...
    That list alone could comprise a *trompe l'œil*
portrait, *à la* Arcimboldo, flickering between
    images of self and loved one never seen
in such a light. A portrait to show me neither boy
    nor man but a captured setting: frozen yet
tropical in turning faces of all things to a light
    that's always held in common, glares for all,
and measures our years in tones that keep on shooting
    past them. A portrait to perform some afterlife of love.

I'd love to paint it, but I can't get further than
    a little clip of her I found online the other day:
a black-and-white Christmas-special episode
    of a children's television show from some time
way before I was born. Wrapped up in a thick
    winter coat and Received Pronunciation, you'd never know
she was used to winters on the other side
    of the world; to a landscape of red earth, bee hives,
shorn sheep, and eucalypts blazing together into
    lengthening December days. The trick
is to be there and not there. It's a pantomime
    she's watching now. I freeze a frame and, yes – I know
her laughter of abandon from my daughter's play.
    A winter solstice midnight is what I am between them.

MY DREAM REALIST NOVEL

For Adam Piette

As this room is a state of want
     Paradise knows he's truant
in a toilet of the School
    of Empathy
               Again

Through a past he didn't live
    he moves   pines
for some voice absorbing earshot

This voice   so cultivated

    packing her own column
    and stigma as an orchid

can only be his distant amazon
    lover   Cathy

         ★

Commercial intimacy is all in the baby
    so Cathy wages her own war
on measure
          Humming
    she makes another living
vehicle of sound
          immaterial labour

    orchid head / doll body /
    reptile limbs

all moving to permutations of clouds
        Paradise tries to copy her hoping
        she will populate him

            ★

Back on the farm sometimes Rupert
        Murdoch sometimes Saddam Hussein
is Paradise's father
              depending on the pollen count

As folds of earth determine a military campaign
        so Nature is complicit in the ambush

Now a hood is face of Rupert
                always a third in Paradise
especially his most utopic voice

            ★

Fiction has shown Cathy
        between the incredible and visible
            lies paper money

Saddam now impossible to see

        Beside himself with Cathy
Paradise embeds infrasonic subwoofer
speakers into things that look like watermelons

        A concentrated avalanche
        of whales
        is what they sound

It's not illness or catastrophes or murders
        that kill and age us
it's the ways people eat laugh and speak

These speakers are to make the captors
        give themselves up quietly

                    ★

Fiction has shown Cathy that Saddam
        sports the immortality of chipper shady
characters who vanish
        and turn up again demanding
loans in cash

Who knows whom Saddam's hostage to?
        Paradise is shitting someone
else's shit
        Finally Cathy quietly loves him for it

                    ★

A unified world must be purely formal?
        Not if she can help it

Another hostage turns commercial and Rupert
is a vast sum of demands
                a catastrophe made nationhood
        a host of female prisoners or weapons
in hard cash

        Cathy's sleeping on it and Paradise
loves her all the more for this

                    ★

The room is a state of illumination
so Paradise knows he's in a greenhouse

    Guards say Saddam escaped it
by draining out to sea   Cathy
    doesn't buy it meaning finally
we're married

Fiction has shown us what we're left with
    is real
Its matter is potentiality
    impressing us to stare
at the blooded inside of our skin
    unawares
This kind of reading forges understanding
we have reached to sleep
    with each other peacefully
as Cathy and I will always now

    so losing our voices

having a whale of a time

ILIAD KID II

A rewriting of Curzio Malaparte's 'Iliade Infantile, II' (1939)

Whether a party of men sets out for dawn
exercises – breaking through windows, seeing
through walls – hangs on tweeted barbs and the day's
      secret blood price.
But you're already running through me
like a play-script, and I feel our garden trembling;
the garden where you hid sweet Grace
      in the form of a soft toy dog.
Your secret is in the number of triangles,
squares, and circles you draw blank as a face
before bursting into a forest of speech,
red and green against the paper sky.
      Gazing into the mirror
of your hand, an immense calm falls
on the garden: the ants are taking stock
like gods, and the birds all sing again
      of Whitney Houston.
Inside, the sweetest forgetting spreads
its Acropolis and the television
is a black marble slab with faintest veins
      of stars.
The world exists only in the blink of an eye.
As that's too brief for breath
we walk through the city
inspired by its armless statues
and mannequins with extra anatomy of pleats
      and zips and buttons.
Too often the anatomy is wrong – especially
at night when a monk's hood announces the Klan
and denounces the day, zipping it up
in a childhood of Charlton Heston,
      Buffalo Bill, or Lone Ranger.

Yet under our garden's bright blank moon
I like to think a better shadow play is cast by rose,
clematis, geranium, rhododendron, banana
plant and weeping fig as all the birds sing
of Helen, Briseïs, Achilles, Hector, Rose
Byrne, Diane Kruger, Brad Pitt, and Eric Bana
        in the same tiny breath.
Then the Aegean will froth about our beds
and all the small fry, gleaming like knives,
will sink deep beneath our marble sleep again.
        At dawn your shoulders
sometimes double as horizon,
and your hand weighs so heavy with veins
        and geography.
All about the city veterans spread their eyes
thinly over things that can't be seen,
while stray adolescents in the woods
and by the river stab up offerings
to their fresh gods: stray cats and dogs
or any other kind of stray.
        O dog head, O Artemis
dog head, O Diane Kruger dog head,
O dog head Muse, O dog head,
I can still hear you barking and howling
the voice of my childhood,
the voice of the woods.
        And so you'll stay,
hidden for later,
somewhere out there in the garden.

OEDIPAL SILVERPOINT RECIPE

Ingredients
½ teaspoon Indigo Powder
2 heaped dessert spoons Ashes of Father
½ cup tap water
1 teaspoon Liquid Gum Arabic
Generous dollop of Zinc White Gouache
1 sheet 200 or 300 gsm Hot-Pressed Paper
1 silver stylus (or see below)

Method
Mix the indigo and father
in a mortar and grind well
with pestle. Slowly trickle in the water,
stirring with a stiff brush until
you have a consistency of thin cream.
Stir in the dollop of white gouache
until ready to conceal any thinking.
Relax: any obstinate blobs of ash
should bind with the gum Arabic –
add it and stir. Now place the paper
on a clean board and moisten its back
with a flat brush dipped in water.
I like Polar White Nylon brushes
for this job because because.
Now, if you find some of the ashes
(bone) remain unbound, it's no loss;
just tweezer them out.
Your mixture should be an incredible
pale grey-blue – as if an iris and the white
of an eye had blended, absorbed its pupil
and spread over the whole globe.
Now turn the paper over.

Take a clean brush and load
it with the prepared mixture
to half-way up from the tip, then apply
it to the paper as your 'ground',
reloading before each stroke. When it's dry,
take a knife and run it around
the paper's edges. You're now ready to draw.
You can use a silver stylus; better still,
I find I give my marks much more
expression by using a few personal
silver souvenirs – a plain hefty ring,
a head-sized hollow Ganesha statue,
and a family fork (excellent for cross-hatching).
Just be mindful before you start that you
can't undo any mark. Decisions, decisions!
(although whatever you draw will be father).
My attempts have all turned out to be a pigeon
sound asleep on its stumps. But after
a few months or so, the silver lines
will have oxidised to a gentle brown –
and so I hope my birds over time
will resemble more a turtle dove. Anyhow,
for now they each make do with 'Untitled'.

CRYOGENIE BLUES

After J. J. Abrams' Cloverfield

this is a hand-held text recording auto-zooming past re-
cordings even if you're headless / a fine film of appetite
over everything / the corner your eye was painted in /
a tail lashing to rain / a baby-shaped rose blancmange
sucked through bic pen barrels / all taste of the same bad
breath? / it may as well be monstrous / latent stem soldiers
/ organ donor kebabs / floating love that hurts without a
loved one / plastic cold war unicorns squared on a saucer
in the kitchen /

              so i rub as every night my 9/11 souvenir
waterglobe / one vehicle from each emergency service
plus confetti / try to rub my cryogenie into being / out-
side now a shush of rain / hands dividing into childhood
as obsolescence / come rain or tail / head or shine / i would
shiver and ask of him / take me away from all this death
/ find i was quoting mina harker in coppola's remake of
dracula / uh oh / something twangling there /

                          now catching
breath / a barely audible sound of holding pitter patterns
/ somewhere cells from the same bone stems are blooming
into both eggs and sperm / once i felt me zoom right out
of ratios / glimpsed a different holding pattern like do-
mestic outer space / only to settle for television hatching
pig-nosed turtle eggs / felt like the right disinterest at the
time /

              soon all cells may be monitored for training pur-
poses / no outside of the sex / fresh orders / not mighty
rationality but rendering of tender meat / held neither
dead nor alive / so much copy running / freezing you in-
side / so kill it into being / feed on down the line / down
the line / no reason but reasons / bundles and bundles of
reasons in the same same breath

MORE BEAUTIFUL THAN A DEAD HORSE

A rewriting of Curzio Malaparte's 'Più bella di un cavallo morto' (1944)

So you're sleeping yet again
    more beautiful than a dead horse
bare arms and long pale thigh
    outflanking patchwork pasture
clenched to new-born souvenir
    and the dead of night
breaking into a snow globe.

Sleep is sparse vegetation for a stomach
    when your city is slowly blowing
up in thin minted air and when you talk
    of this you seem resigned to graze
on fields of snow. Eating from ground up
    is best way to turn the horizon vertical
as a monument to all those horizontal.

Just thinking as I'm talking is also
    a powerful fantasy like natural rhythm
and you can't possess a body without it.
    Slight sound of an oar against the shore-
line opposite makes another horizon.
    Mountains moaning surrounded by black
firs also are a sleep against the shore-line.

By 'natural' do we still wheel on the 'national'
    concealed inside a Trojan mare?
I dream of being everywhere –
    spend my days encouraging the moss
and lichens growing over toes

and ears of statues to assume the whole
knackered body.

What the thunder says in here is free-floating
    hunger straight from the horse's head:
What bed do I leave this in?
    Or I simply ask to be all over
just the city that's your city
    as a rise and fall is breathing
in your city.

EUCALYPSO REDUX

I *10 JULY*

A week I am in this hotel of indecision
    with its single fan musing how sweet it were
a helicopter waiting for a mission. Blades
    chop the building rush of dark internal river
to a mirror fitting like the best fatigues.
    When I touch it flashes blanks of finger-
prints before they are submerged below a plush rose
    tide. Mr Quartz may be resting dead in line
to be a private plot of park or maybe just
    a studio – all I know is this plot must be
mine. I must *have* it in all senses.
    I'm sick of filling hollow space with booze
and food and air – here where the public garden's
    riot falls so quick to quiet.

II *11 JULY*

Now we're punting down a sequence of dolly-
    shots and flashbacks called the Cam – dragonflies
zipping frames in the air all about us.
    At present Quartz is just an occasional scent
of Paris – arresting red wine kidneys pavement –
    that settles hot on us a blush. I know he's broken
contact to be shameful – that old mode of male
    pregnancy again. 'Shame is a beach
under the paving stones' – and if his story's a confession
    we are all in it together. He once showed me a cartoon
mural of a cow airlifted by helicopter sighing 'Ah,
    la vie.' It was on earth as it was in heaven –
that state of affairs we call a restaurant.
    Neither piety nor pity.

III *13 JULY*

The silence in our experience is growing Tasmaniacal —
    broken only by the odd bee bursting
kazoo electric snickers in some floating lotos.
    Sounds like the essence of violence to me.
Actinomorphic revolute reflexed — we're surrounded
    by states of teasels nettles brambles umbels.
Let us alone! or give us at least as camouflage
    consistency of cuckoo spit. The sheltered being
sheds limits to his shelter and when expectation
    feels a kind of circus tent let us mistrust
the staunchest trees. I read more of Quartz's dossier —
    he trod down several strange paths and gods
only to live cruelly with a man he might have been.
    It feels like he is living *anywhere*.

IV *14 JULY*

Somewhere along the way he missed the sexual
    turn-off, the secret brighter coloured life of organs.
So he began performing speechless contortions
    for passers-by who had to visualise this internal
circus of intestines folded flipped and sorely tried.
    He calls these trials 'TONE'
but silent workings of his face are all we have
    to go on. I'm getting *jamais vu* again –
we must be getting close. His eyes rise up
    unbearable and might be seen to say 'My beauty
you may not sustain. I am beef and you
    are my pet lamb devoid of blindfold
at the carneval. Call me a better Abraham...

V 14 JULY (CONT.)

... take on board my propositions:
    I break contact so you can be my pain
while I protect you from the pain. That way
    labour reverts to pregnancy again.
I call this going into partnership.
    I couldn't get no sacrifaction – in the 'couldn't'
felt my love grow unconditional again.
    No one else right now is having *this* pain
and that is true for good.
    Any murder charges are insane
but I worry that my pain won't understand.
    Your feet and hands are they not strong?
Can they not stand for swathes of grass and pavement?
    That trembling underneath your skin...

VI *15 JULY*

... mere inoculation also known as *perseverity*.'
    He falls to one more sequence of contortions.
Now I see this river its becoming running deep
    inside. It's like I'm in a tent that moves
the muscles of my eyes. I see this taut
    suspension was the mission.
It's like I'm in a tent of muscle
    ripped and toned so I can almost take
his heart into my own.
    My naked body now is one big face
of camouflage composed of river scene –
    reflexed revolute actinomorphic –
and with a slew of credits running through it
    so I vanish. For what you leave well remains.

100 YEARS SUSPENDED IN WAR

save the sum of eyes for pay
give us time that doesn't count
shoulders holding sky suspended
each one bearing its half life
in the frieze before his eyes
hanging silent on her words
as if consciousness existed
in the time it takes to draft
a column's dying crux of hope
night a fur you can afford
any moment sealed in post
all that 'giveup' time to audit
given glimpse of guilt to bury
surrendered blankness of our sleep
beyond recall for harmless streets
hanging silent in her words
the last white bulldog of that breed
completely reconciled to life
in time it takes to change the channel
in the form of wild bravado
given time that doesn't count
in psychoanalytic sessions
rising foam of quickened breath
peals of laughter from the jungle
gaping margins of the sea
leave me free to live and write

back to what may have been home
leave them happier on reflection
hardened fast to black cement
less a house and more a pause
could have given her address
without a proper blood supply

as if they made spontaneous work
the guarantee of changeless love
turning into drops of rain
persisting even old or maimed
completely reconciled to life
less a pause and more a house
for a 'new limb' waiting there
the guarantee of changeless love
whistling to the peals of laughter
bank to shell and fly to amber
partitioned off from universe
a child again if birth there is
survived intact from ancient Greece
as if the worst would be to kill him
with bunting dolls and avocados
the guarantee of changeless love
a frozen tank in frozen mud
as if that side of brain closed up
give us daily pause for sleep
Achilles' heel Achilles' shield!
save the sum of eyes for pay
xylophone to telescope
as if a tuning fork were struck
turning into drops of rain
light bulbs set in hand grenades
a radar screen of souvenirs
I couldn't make up proper notes
not worth writing home about
facial freeze to hairline crack
seeing how I must have loved her
could have tipped the odds of history
living in my father's body

as if consciousness existed
zooming panning round the streets
to hammer home again again
fifty feet by fifty feet
the guarantee of changeless love
they left and so were never here
completely reconciled to life
save the sum of eyes for pay
surrendered blankness of our sleep
a rush of river livid sky
fifty feet by fifty feet
dark spots tracking into desert
carried past in memories crossing
at home and war at the same time
whole time being slowly counting
half a blacksmith's shop inside her
long to feel myself the column
leave to make myself believe

in time it takes to pull the trigger
partitioned off from universe
felt magnetic plot effect
collapsing features leaves a stare
under skin between the sheets
the times I could have proved my worth
with metal leaves and café tables
bunting dolls and avocados
a deer gone for a drink to creek
as if perception drifts away
tender limbs organic shrapnel
live blimp-cam video feed
leaves a certain taste in mouth
as if they each hold half a life
bank at shell and fly to amber
as a new limb waiting there
Achilles' heel Achilles' shield
the guarantee of changeless love

JUDITH AND HOLOFERNES

Even integrity can fall to a skin of wine
        emptying itself legs apart, and her decision –
a helmetful of breathlessness –
        her decision is bronze as falchion,
lace, and shoulder-blade are bronze,
        for suspension is a kind of conscience
cast as solid ghost to execute it.
        Then the city must be substituted
for a canvas tent with many paintings
        nailed in check by other names and frames.
For Cranach she's an exoskeleton or piecrust
        crimped into knuckles, slashed and serene,
while his head is filling with giblets of city
        cut-out. She has saved up her gaze
from the past – from when Mantegna's tent offered
        her labour so oblivious she saw through
his head, staring away at nothing,
        a deserted foot sole also of a piece
with integrity. This prepares us to conceive
        how his painted head is really the artist's head –
which is why she holds it blithely as a pineapple
        ripe for a trolley in Allori's version.
Shadow too is a kind of news packaging,
        which brings us naturally to the hard labour
that's gone into any head, and here Caravaggio
        makes an entrance. Heaven is a burgundy
velvet canopy where she is pulling a small face
        of earth into something neither by-standing
nor understanding, her handmaid waiting to bag it.
        Even when the eyes go out, vision can live
on blood. So Gentileschi saw in painting it
        a spray of tamarisk,
                fire-adapted,

propagating through cuttings, long tap-roots
intercepting deep water-tables of revenge
            and victory. For the future is blood
as form of speed, as form of fibre-optic.

ON BALANCE

For my daughter, aged 2

Morning is a family trip to a troglodyte city
    of caves to picture how the Neolithics
were always between a rock and hard
    people. I take a long shot
of you looking minute out to hills and river –
    it looks as though the cave is set to chew
you into view. When you let the camera drop
    our faces fall. Some instant distance never stops
feeling like the more you
    try to cross it sadly it will never
let you bridge it. No wonder humans rarely dwell long out-
    side of rectangles these days. Then we remembered
the nearby zoo's endangered kebabs ('Susliks'?)
    and fell back to making up our trogloditty

about those birds that looked like massive dusky muscatels.
    Caves, trees, clouds, trucks, snakes,
birds, lily pads, dragonflies, fish –
    is it because they seem never to fall
that you have so much time for these things?
    I think a soul, like a snake, is only the matter
that's living *as* it: precarious, innocent, irrevocable, enveloping
    what it's not until it seems there's no stopping
the little life it stretches to. Think of water
    scattering like mercury into tiny quivering
mutable lenses that make up more than its total
    when dropped onto a lotus leaf. Think of the flash
of astonishment in Poussin's *Landscape with a Man Killed by a Snake* –
    how the man recoiling at the scene repeats in muscles

of his limbs the undulations of corpse and snake.
    By evening the morning's changed into a primal
scene: you surrounding your own falls with comic walk;
    a sifaka monkey in flouncy pyjamas
prancing round a trampoline. A red kite circling its chance
    as lizards ampersand the sun for shade.
I don't pray like Yeats that you'll turn out to be
    someone with thoughts like a 'linnet'; someone who's a 'hidden tree'.
I just hope you'll keep throwing yourself open as water made
    more gifted, more charismatic, by its accidence.
Beware those who bare their daily dramas
    as a shelf-life or endless exile of the face. Beware any talk
of despair: every body harbours ways of balancing what's truly dismal
    with a bouncing off the day that never breaks.

[NOTE TO SELFIE-DRONE]

★ [throw her into *Boomerang* mode so up
she'll hover follow me] [here I am
yes here I am clear symptoms
Exeter of the face] [must be in love
with all the cannots] [must be
an interface] [raw format sun
its fail-safe setting] [cost a cluster
as in people] [numbersome so
numbersome] ★ [track to capture
best flipside] [backside of face
we call a head] [all its look of unawares
its look of *never saw it coming*]
[zero in hands-free unmanned]
[flashback tones] [*target-
follow*] [hands-free to snap
my *flying Fuckface*] [double-fledged
feed breaking up] ★ [we're here
together in Chernobyl] [together yet
so out of reach] [a clip shot
in child setting] [hands-free and so
unbearable] ★ [*Smile & Obstacle
Recognition Software*] [sometimes
seeing one as other] [Abrahamming]
[Kierkegaarding] [here I'm panned
on Gog Magog hill battling Bury
of the face] [*2-axis gimbal* centering]
[hands-free and so unborne]
★ [off she goes up *Boomerang*
so every head is shot with silence]
[secret is the substitute] [hands-free to keep
it to itself] [you can't stand past the top
of a hill yet over and over she hovers

above it] [smiling with all there was
between us] [peanut camera
Bluetooth platform] [a backside smile
that came between us] [*flying interFuckface*
setting] ★ [*flying interFuckface*
trigger] [*flying interFuckface*
backflash] [here I wonder at the secret]
[caught in time with impersona] [secrecy
is substitution] [keep it open for
my daughter] [do my best to keep her
from it] ★ [sequenced numbersome head
refraining] [latest footage Cambridge head]
[not Datakhel not Mount Moriah]
[not Creech Nevada nor Wara Dara]
[not Sana'a nor Zinjibar] ★ [my own
pattern lucky life] [dear outer
heart] [must learn to fly new
unmanned face] [our secret makes
its substitution] [there we are now
here we are] [learn to keep
her close to me] [hands-
free so open to unbear
me] [here I am yes
here I am] [yes
here I am
yes *here*] ★

ACKNOWLEDGEMENTS

First and foremost to Vahni Capildeo for her encourage-
ment, support, and advice over the last few years, and
for her wise comments on the full draft of this volume:
grazie mille, Vahnissima! I have also benefited from get-
ting intoxicated frequently on the poetic intelligences of
Matthew Bevis, Geoffrey Gilbert, Adam Piette, and Anne
Stillman. A number of other people have offered me kind
encouragements and support over recent years: in particu-
lar, Kelvin Corcoran, Peter Hughes, John Kinsella, Rod
Mengham, Drew Milne, Maureen N. McLane, Ian Patter-
son, Peter Riley, Todd Swift, and Khadija von Zinnenburg
Carroll – my hearty thanks to you all.

I am grateful to the editors of the following publications
in which some of the poems in this collection appeared,
often in somewhat different form: *Best New British and
Irish Poets 2016* (Eyewear, 2016); *Rouge States* (Oystercatcher,
2014); *face down in the book of revelations* (Oystercatcher, 2016);
Sheffield Anthology (Smith/Doorstop, 2012); *Poetry London*;
PN Review; *The Wolf Magazine*; *Shearsman Magazine*;
Counter Text; *Cambridge Literary Review*; *Stand Magazine*;
Fortnightly Review; *3AM*; *Molly Bloom*; *Cordite*; *Free Verse*;
Stride; *Great Works*; and *Horizon Review*.

The illustrations of the dog with carnival mask and pigeon
on its stumps are by me.

My thanks to the Eyewear team, particularly the director,
Todd Swift, the managing editor, Alexandra Payne, and
designer, Edwin Smet, for all the fine work they've put
into producing *Ring Cycle*.

This book is dedicated to my daughter, Isabella.

EYEWEAR PUBLISHING

EYEWEAR
POETRY

TITLES INCLUDE

ELSPETH SMITH DANGEROUS CAKES
CALEB KLACES BOTTLED AIR
GEORGE ELLIOTT CLARKE ILLICIT SONNETS
HANS VAN DE WAARSENBURG THE PAST IS NEVER DEAD
BARBARA MARSH TO THE BONEYARD
DON SHARE UNION
SHEILA HILLIER HOTEL MOONMILK
MARION MCCREADY TREE LANGUAGE
SJ FOWLER THE ROTTWEILER'S GUIDE TO THE DOG OWNER
AGNIESZKA STUDZINSKA WHAT THINGS ARE
JEMMA BORG THE ILLUMINATED WORLD
KEIRAN GODDARD FOR THE CHORUS
COLETTE SENSIER SKINLESS
ANDREW SHIELDS THOMAS HARDY LISTENS TO LOUIS ARMSTRONG
JAN OWEN THE OFFHAND ANGEL
A.K. BLAKEMORE HUMBERT SUMMER
SEAN SINGER HONEY & SMOKE
HESTER KNIBBE HUNGERPOTS
MEL PRYOR SMALL NUCLEAR FAMILY
ELSPETH SMITH KEEPING BUSY
TONY CHAN FOUR POINTS FOURTEEN LINES
MARIA APICHELLA PSALMODY
TERESE SVOBODA PROFESSOR HARRIMAN'S STEAM AIR-SHIP
ALICE ANDERSON THE WATERMARK
BEN PARKER THE AMAZING LOST MAN
ISABEL ROGERS DON'T ASK
REBECCA GAYLE HOWELL AMERICAN PURGATORY
MARION MCCREADY MADAME ECOSSE
MARIELA GRIFFOR DECLASSIFIED
MARK YAKICH THE DANGEROUS BOOK OF POETRY FOR PLANES
HASSAN MELEHY A MODEST APOCALYPSE
KATE NOAKES PARIS, STAGE LEFT
JASON LEE BURNING BOX
U.S. DHUGA THE SIGHT OF A GOOSE GOING BAREFOOT
TERENCE TILLER THE COLLECTED POEMS
MATTHEW STEWART THE KNIVES OF VILLALEJO
PAUL MULDOON SADIE AND THE SADISTS
JENNA CLAKE FORTUNE COOKIE
TARA SKURTU THE AMOEBA GAME
MANDY KAHN GLENN GOULD'S CHAIR
CAL FREEMAN FIGHT SONGS
TIM DOOLEY WEEMOED
MATTHEW PAUL THE EVENING ENTERTAINMENT
NIALL BOURKE DID YOU PUT THE WEASELS OUT?
USHA KISHORE IMMIGRANT
DUSTIN PEARSON MILLENIAL ROOST
LEAH UMANSKY THE BARBAROUS CENTURY
STEVE KRONEN HOMAGE TO MISTRESS OPPENHEIMER
FAISAL MOHYUDDIN THE DISPLACED CHILDREN OF DISPLACED CHILDREN